VENTURE!

A SIMPLE GUIDE TO HELP YOU SURVIVE YOUR FIRST YEAR IN BUSINESS

GATHONI NJENGA

Copyright © 2019 Ostrich Publishers

All rights reserved.

ISBN: 9781087287683

DID YOU KNOW?

That according to the Small Business Association (SBA), 50% of new businesses fail within the first five years? The SBA also states that only 25% make it to 15 years or more.

DEDICATIONS

To all the small business owners, the pave-pounders, the stay-up-all nighters. Here is to you!

CONTENTS

Introduction	Reasons Startups Fail	11
Chapter 1	Good leaders make good followers	26
Chapter 2	Been in business for a while and still making no money? Don't worry, it's normal	35
Chapter 3	Skip the office space, for now	46
Chapter 4	Looks like we need a plan	58
Chapter 5	Raising capital for your startup	75
Chapter 6	Do not overlook these hidden startup costs	90
Chapter 7	Build a Team Around You	100
Chapter 8	Improve on The Idea	116
Chapter 9	Be Sure to Consult the Consultants	126
Chapter 10	Here is what you need	133

Bonus	158
Afterword	166
Notes	175

VENTURE: A SIMPLE GUIDE TO HELP YOU SURVIVE YOUR FIRST YEAR IN BUSINESS

INTRODUCTION

REASONS WHY STARTUPS FAIL

Failure is never easy. Heck, for most people, just the thought of crashing and burning is the main reason they never take risks or try new things. Fear of failure is the No. 1 reason people don't set goals or explore new opportunities. A recent survey by the social network Linkagoal found that fear of failure plagued 31% of 1,083 adult respondents — a larger percentage than those who feared spiders (30%), being home alone (9%) or even the paranormal (15%).

People are terrified of failing at things. However, believe it or not, failure is part of life. Talk to any successful person you know, and they will tell you how many times they have landed on their face trying to accomplish something. I actually think failure, when handled correctly is an important component of one's ultimate success, whatever that may be.

Every time you fail at something, you have an opportunity to gain some insight on how not to approach future endeavors. If we learn to deal with our failures in constructive ways, we can learn to build effective systems around the knowledge we extrapolate from our failures.

The best things in life aren't free

Anything worth having in life takes hard work. This is a fact of life I have come to accept. Nothing comes easy. Your new business will be no different. You will spend countless hours working on building your business. Before it's all said and done, you will have thrown everything you have at it. You will stretch yourself so thin, go so far out of your comfort zone that you will sometimes wonder if it's all worth it.

I bring this up just to let you know that in order to succeed, you are going to work harder than what your perception of hard work is. But this is ok, right? because you are ready to take this journey, correct? Before you commit to doing this, I need you to get your head in the game. I need you to know the very few succeed at what you are trying to do. This ain't gonna be easy. But you know what? You can do it.

Based on the results of a survey of 101 businesses conducted by CB Insights, these are the top 5 reasons why Small Businesses Fail.

#1: No market need

Tackling problems that are interesting to solve rather than those that serve a market need was cited as the No. 1 reason for failure, noted in 42% of cases. It is therefore imperative that any new business takes the time and dedicate the resources needed to conduct a thorough market study.

Solution:

Make sure that you are able to identify and quantify a real need in the marketplace for your product or service. I won't go into the "big enough" issue. Why? Because I don't think there is one universal answer to this question. Is the market big enough? Well, that depends on what big enough means to your business. I think each entrepreneur ought to determine for themselves whether any market need is sizable enough for them and what that means for their business.

"Startups fail when they are not solving a market problem. We were not solving a large enough problem that we could universally serve with a scalable solution. We had great technology, great data on shopping behavior, great reputation as a thought leader, great expertise, great advisors,

etc., but what we didn't have was technology or business model that solved a pain point in a scalable way."

#2: Ran out of cash

Money and time are finite and need to be allocated judiciously. The question of how you should spend your money was a frequent conundrum and reason for failure cited by startups (29%).

Solution:

Here is a topic I talk about all the time. Surprisingly, this is one most new business owners and entrepreneurs, I feel don't pay enough attention to. The truth is, you are going to need money to start and grow your business.

If for nothing else, you are going to have to pay yourself a salary and devote tons of cash to marketing. You have to let as many people as possible know about your product and that is going to take money. So, you need to go out and get some.

You will have to plan and forecast all your expected

expenses for your first 12-24 months in business, and then try to get the funding you need. You can use your savings, find Angel investors, friends, and family, etc. I will get into all this in a later chapter.

As the team at Flud exemplified, running out of cash was often tied to other reasons for startup failure including failure to find product-market fit and failed pivots.

"In fact, what eventually killed Flud was that the company wasn't able to raise this additional funding. Despite multiple approaches and incarnations in pursuit of the ever-elusive product-market fit (and monetization), Flud eventually ran out of money — and a runway."

#3: Not on the right team

A diverse team with different skill sets was often cited as being critical to the success of a company. Failure post-mortems often lamented that "I wish we had a CTO from the start," or wished that the startup had "a founder that loved the business aspect of things." In some cases, the founding team wished they had more checks and balances. As Nouncer's founder wrote, "This brings me back to the underlying problem I didn't have a partner to balance me out and provide sanity checks for business and technology decisions made."

Solution:

In the coming chapters, I will talk in great detail about the importance of building a strong, competent, cohesive team around you. For the sake of your business and all who depend on you, it is very important that you do not bring people on to join your team simply because you know or like them. Your founding team needs to be packed with folks who have a special set of expertise to fulfill all the detrimental aspects of your company. Other than being able to see the big picture and build teams themselves, most, if not all of your founding members have to occupy an irreplaceable space in the company ecosystem. You need a salesperson, a financial guy or gal - one who has relationships with wealthy individuals and financial institutions and has experience raising money for a startup. You need an "ideas person", and you need a manager. The one who can tie this whole thing together.

#4: Fierce Competition

Despite the platitudes that startups shouldn't pay attention to the competition, the reality is that once an idea gets hot or gets market validation, there may be many entrants in a space. And while obsessing over the competition is not healthy, ignoring them was also a recipe for failure in 19% of the startup failures.

Solution:

It helps for Startup founders to keep an eye on any existing or potential competitors. My take? You want to make a list of all your competitors and ones that you think might popup once your business gains traction. What I have done in the past is, I have made a list of all the things we as a company can do to differentiate ourselves from the competition. I will give you an example. About a year ago I noticed a startup coffee shop in my neighborhood. Now, I thought this was a great idea because I lived in a part of town, perhaps the only part of Charlotte, NC. That had no coffee shops at all. I kid you not. No Starbucks, Panera, nothing, for about 10 miles.

So, I went into this cute new coffee shop. I talked to the owner for a while. I must admit, I thought this would be a good investment. I actually shared my thoughts with her, and she was open to the idea, knowing she could use a few extra bucks to spruce up the place and stock up on supplies.

I had one stipulation though; I required that we get a license to sell alcohol and add a wine bar to the location. She immediately refused. " I want this to be a place for Coffee lovers only. I want to sell many kinds of Coffee, but no alcohol", she said. So, I told her it made no sense to invest if she was not willing to add, at the very least wine to her offerings. We went back and forth for a while and she later told me that this was a deal-breaker for her, and I agreed it was for me too. Then she asked why this was such a big deal to me.

So, I told her. My take? It would only be a matter of time till one of the big coffee chains catches wind of all the money we are making here and decides they want a piece of the action. I told her, Now I know Starbucks or Panera will not change their corporate identity just for one little location, so they will not sell alcohol, thereby leaving us to handle the folks who want a little something extra with their coffee. I also recommended, no insisted that we stay open past 9 pm. Needless to say, she refused that as well. Six months later, I noticed a "Coming soon" sign with the unmistakable green Mermaid logo on it. Yup, Starbucks was moving in.

She has since closed her Coffee shop and

Starbucks is making a killing in the neighborhood. Plan for all scenarios having to do with competition. If you are left alone to keep making money, that's great but chances are, if you make a dollar, folks will want their cut.

#5: Pricing / Cost issues

Pricing is a dark art when it comes to startup success, and startup post-mortems highlight the difficulty in pricing a product high enough to eventually cover costs but low enough to bring in customers.

Solution:

There are two ways in which I have approached the issue of pricing in previous ventures. You have to ask yourself where you fit into the overall marketplace. Are you looking to be a lower-priced solution? The Walmart approach, or do you want to offer a product at a premium with higher quality and world-class customer service? More like Apple Inc?

Be sure to take these questions into consideration, along with the important goal of making a profit while paying your overhead costs. Trying to figure out what to charge for your offerings should not be fueled by ego or deluded sense of self, but rather, this should be a well-thought-out process that will, hopefully, attract customers.

#6: Poor Marketing / Sales

Knowing your target audience and knowing how to get their attention and convert them to leads and ultimately customers is one of the most important skills of a successful business. But an inability to market was a common failure especially among founders who liked to code or build a product but who didn't relish the idea of promoting the product.

Solution:

Whether you like it or not, you are a Salesperson. You are a Marketer. Just the thought of interacting with others to sell them something makes most of us uncomfortable, but it is what it is. You are in sales. If you wish to grow your business, before you have the budget to hire and train a sales team, you need to figure out how you are going to get the word out about your offerings. You will have to build a well-oiled system around sales and marketing.

Please resist the temptation to hire an outside marketing firm. This may seem like a good idea at the time, but this strategy never works out. Not when you are first starting your company. Take matters into your own hands. After all, these subcontractors do not have the level of passion that you do about your products and services. Even if you are able to work with them to build an effective sales machine, you know they will just turn around and sell that service to your competitors. Try to control every aspect of your sales apparatus to ensure profits as soon as possible.

There are many reasons why Startup businesses fail

Here in this chapter, I have tried to highlight a few. The ones I deem most common and I have provided some ideas as to what I think the solution to some of these issues are. These suggestions are merely based on my experience gained during the launching of over five businesses. Over the years, I have learned that successfully starting a business is like predicting rain: There are many ways to try to predict the outcome, but ultimately, you could do everything right and still face some significant obstacles.

The key is to plan for every possible eventuality and have methods and systems to traverse each hurdle. To give yourself a greater chance at success, you want to (a) Have a solid sales and marketing plan, (b) Build a competent team around you, (c)

Have a capital or fundraising plan, and (d) Conduct thorough market research to help price your products and services appropriately and plan to deal with your existing and potential competitors.

CHAPTER ONE

Good leaders make good followers

Warren Buffett was once a paper delivery boy. *Oprah*

Winfrey *started her working life as a Grocery Store Clerk.* ***Michael Bloomberg*** *was once a Parking Lot Attendant.* ***Jeff Bezos'*** *first job was Grill operator at McDonald's. Bottom line is, some of the world's richest and most successful people were once employees themselves.*

I don't like people telling me what to do

It never ceases to amaze me how often I hear entrepreneurs say that they started or are looking to start a business because they are tired of people telling them what to do. " I want to be my own boss; I don't want anyone telling me what to do". I mean, I get the whole empowerment and self-determination vibe. I feel as though that for most people it's an ego thing.

I say this because usually if you keep talking to this type of person about their previous or current employment situation, you will soon find out that they either were or are a terrible employee. It almost never fails. They are usually indifferent to their position and will typically know nothing or care to know anything about the companies they work for, the people they work with, or the product and/or service they put out into the marketplace.

They often lack passion for their jobs. The idea is "Hey, this is not my company so what do I care? I will be more inspired once I have my own company". The truth is, things don't actually work this way. To be successful in business, you will have to tap into some very personal values. Once that a less self-aware person who lacks often doesn't realize it. I am talking about discipline, team spirit, attention to detail, punctuality, the ability to create systems, consistency, etc. All qualities we master while working for someone else.

We Can't all be like Mark

Sure, there are folks who have never worked for anyone and went on to be very successful. Mark Zuckerberg is obviously one of them. If you have been living under a rock for the past fifteen years, then let me provide some color: Mark Elliot Zuckerberg, the Facebook founder, and CEO started the Social media giant with his college roommates, Eduardo Saverin, Andrew McCollum, Dustin Moskovitz, and Chris Hughes out of their Harvard dorm room. He was only 20 years old at the time. History books and financial media often tell tales of very young people launching billion-dollar companies almost overnight. You know, the ones who never had to work for "The man" and therefore never took crap from anyone.

Although there are some folks who just struck gold right out of the gate, the truth is, these stories, in the grand scheme of things, are less frequent than you might think. Yeah sure, if you are an entrepreneur at heart, you have always felt this way. You always know that the 9-5 thing was not for you, and I get that, but most people who are like you, took that desire and went into the workforce. Working passionately to develop their skills. Heck, some even got their former bosses to help them start their own businesses.

Others worked on their companies while working for someone else. Jeff Bezos started working on Cadabra, the company that he would later call Amazon while he worked at D. E. Shaw.

Follow good leaders

I have a friend who works at one of the largest Mutual fund companies in America. As I search my mind, it seems like Bob has been with this Valley Forge, PA. Company forever. To say he has climbed the corporate ladder over the last ten years would be an understatement. He has moved up to a better position almost every year, it seems. I kid you not. The thing is, he actually started at the bottom with this firm. But now he has really moved up. Meanwhile, he has also managed to build a substantial portfolio of residential real estate properties.

By all accounts, my friend Bob is winning at life. I asked him once, over a cup of coffee, the reason behind his upward mobility. He told me that, among other things, he found a mentor within the company. Someone in upper management who took on the responsibility of helping him develop his leadership skills and to push him towards every single new opportunity within the firm that fits into his overall planned trajectory. Do you see where I am going with this? Bob has accomplished and continues to pursue his dreams both in and outside his job because he is learning from a good leader. I often advise entrepreneurs to seek out great leaders, even at their 9-5, and learn from them. Find someone you respect, but more importantly, one in upper management who is good at their jobs.

Folks in upper management don't just work for the company, they run it. They are essentially businesspeople themselves. Learn everything you can from them, even while you lay the groundwork to launch your own company.

Know thyself

It's funny how the longer you do something, the more you find out about yourself. Or is it just me? Before I went into business for myself, I spent years in the corporate world doing the 9-5 thing. I worked for many different companies in various industries. I swear, with each position I learned something new about myself. At the Olive Garden, I found out how much I love interacting with people but hated the smell of old food. OnStar was a pain because I really did not like being cooped up in an office all day. I discovered my love of sales while working for All-State. Plus, I have always loved traveling and always knew I wanted to be well compensated for whatever I ended up doing.

Armed with all this knowledge and insights about my own personality, I charged right into the world of financial services. I was an Independent Financial Adviser for a while. This was when I met the man that would later become my husband. He was in the same industry as well, well sort of. While I was associated with a large firm, he had launched his own practice. So, when I left my firm, (we were dating at the time) I thought it best to join his firm.

Through the ups and downs, today we have grown our little company into one that extends into real estate, I.T Services, eCommerce, and publishing. Point being, working for someone else can help you discover who you are and what you want to do when you go into business for yourself.

A system for this, and a system for that

If you have ever worked for a company in the past or are currently employed by a corporation, then I am pretty sure you did, or currently work with systems all day long. You may have never given it much thought before. Every organization, to be successful needs to design and implement efficient systems. When I say systems, I am referring to the well-established, well-defined processes through which various important functions of a business are completed.

The marketing department has a set of repeatable, teachable systems. Systems are everything. I urge you to look to your time in the workforce to figure out how to build solid systems for your business. You should have systems for sales, customer support, customer on-boarding, etc. Be sure to create detailed training manuals for each system. Google Drive it and save it. Go back and make changes once you gain some more experience running your firm. You will be able to use these documented systems to train new employees once you start hiring.

CHAPTER TWO

Been in business for a while and still making no money? Don't worry, it's normal

Let me explain.

Before I jump into this topic, I would like to clarify what I mean by " Money". Money, in this context, refers to profits: What you make after you have paid all overhead expenses. Your earnings before interest, taxes, depreciation, and amortization, or **EBITDA**. So, I wouldn't dare suggest that you expect to earn no revenue during the first years of your business, and if this is the case with your business, then you might have to address some fundamental issues with your business model. It surprises most folks I spoke to hear that some of America's most iconic brands went for a while without profits.

How long does it take for a business to make a profit?

This is a question we hear entrepreneurs ask all the time. Perhaps, this is one that you are currently pondering yourself. Most of us go into business, if for the first time, with lofty expectations. Expectations that typically have very little basis in reality, but rather fueled by emotions and blind pursuit of success.

The reality is, profitability is somewhat of a distant goal, for any business. Did you know that all things being equal, it takes the average startup anywhere from 2 - 3 years to show a profit? Amazon operated at a loss for most of its history. It would take Facebook 5 years to book a small profit, a milestone the company cleared in 2009.

So you see, when starting a new business, you have to plan to operate at a loss for at least the first two years, and thus all your planning should reflect and layout a plan to fund the business while you grow your customer base and formulate out your brand identity.

You are in good company

FedEx

Founded in 1962 by Frederick W. Smith, the giant overnight-delivery company struggled at first to take off. In fact, FedEx at one point was on the verge of bankruptcy. In a crazy twist, Smith flew to Vegas, where he played Blackjack with the firm's last $5000. He won $24000, which he used to cover FedEx's overhead to keep the company going. The company made its first profit in July 1975. Today, the Memphis-based company enjoys a total revenue of more than $3 billion.

Amazon

So, you know, I talk about Amazon a lot because I love the company, plus I feel the company its founder is the best representation of the entrepreneurial story. We all know the story of how Bezos left his well-paying job on Wall Street to go sell Books online. He set up shop in his garage and by 1997 Amazon was bringing in $147.8 million in annual revenue. The company reached revenues of $1.6 billion in 1999 but still managed to take a loss of $719 million that same year. The company finally turned a profit in 2003, which was nine years after being founded and seven years after going public.

Tesla Motors

Founded as an Electric car company by Martin Eberhard and Marc Tarpenning in 2003, and later taken over by Elon Musk. In 2009, Tesla received a "$465 million USD loan from the United States Department of Energy" and went public the following year. However, it wasn't until 2013 (a decade after its launch) that Tesla experienced its first profitable quarter, ever.

ESPN

Founded in 1979 as an all-sports Network by father-and-son team, Bill and Scott Rasmussen, with the help of Aetna insurance agent Ed Eagan. The company's model was simple; create content that sports fans will love. Yes, the idea was simple. Running the business? Not so much. ESPN struggled financially for a while.

To help keep ESPN going, Michael Roarty (vice president and director of marketing for Anheuser-Busch) persuaded the brewing company to financially support the struggling network. In 1994, Roarty told the St. Louis Post-Dispatch, "We gave them $1 million that first year. And if we hadn't, they'd have gone under." The following year, Anheuser-Busch gave ESPN an additional $5 million. By the mid-1980s, ESPN was able to turn a profit thanks to the support of Anheuser-Busch.

The American corporate universe is littered with stories like these. Unbeknownst to the average person, most startups, even with a widely used product or service often struggle to make a profit. This is no reason to be discouraged. What you want to do is to have a solid plan on how to raise additional capital while working to increase sales and reduce cost. That's how you become profitable.

Setting yourself up for success

The best thing you can do to start the planning process for your new business is to clearly identify what you consider "profitability" to be. Will you consider your business profitable when you can pay all expenses plus yourself? Or will you say you are profitable at a point when you can pay all expenses, plus tax, payroll, and put a little bit in the bank? This question is important as it will help you know how to set up your financial models.

To set yourself up for success, I recommend taking the time to write out a detailed business plan. Be sure to include any outside funds you would like to raise. I also strongly recommend having 2 pitch sheets, one for yourself and your team, and the other for potential investors or strategic partners.

The internal one should go into detail about how you plan to grow your business plus any proprietary advantages you may have. The other should just give a broad overview of your mission, vision, and plan.

Financial forecasting

Others may disagree with me on this, but I value your financial forecasting/pro forma above all other planning documents. For me, here is where I get to see if I can invest in a business idea or not. Oh, I should also mention that I do not like to start any venture without knowing I can piece together the funding (initially and ongoing) till profitability. But that's just me. I do not like Hail Mary situations in business.

Here, it is best to create various scenarios for cash flow, revenues (starting at $0), future loans, outside investments, etc. Take inventory of how you will fund this business until it is able to stand on its own.
Using Live Plan to build these financial models is the best way to go. For $20/mo. you will have access to the company's powerful business planning tools.

Measuring Profitability

There are three ways to measure profitability: for the principals, for the investors and for the business as a whole. Consider the hypothetical case of an entrepreneur who leaves a $50,000 salaried job to start a business. In the first year, the business clears

$125,000, which becomes the entrepreneur's salary.

The business as a whole shows no profit, as that salary is another business expense, but the entrepreneur she has profited well from the startup. Likewise, payments to investors can be structured so they're earning interest even when the business is officially breaking even or losing money.

You really need to have a marketing plan

Start out with a solid, practical plan on how you will get the word out to your prospective customers about your products and services. After carefully analyzing your market and clearly identifying your target audience, i.e. who in the marketplace consumes products like yours or could benefit from your offering. Not who you would like to buy your product. You want to map out a multi-platform marketing campaign approach.

If your target audience is younger, then you want

to invest most of your resources to communicate your value proposition via digital marketing. Building a robust social media and email campaign strategy is the best way to go here.

Mailers and just straight-up calling people up works with an older, more rural audience. Yes, people out in the country still talk on phones. Be prepared to invest heavily in marketing, and I advise having several types of marketing campaigns running simultaneously at all times. Adjust your financial forecasting to cover the cost of marketing on an ongoing basis. In a later chapter, I will go a little deeper into the need and the importance of making detailed plans. I will also provide some resources to help you set up the various plans you will need to help grow your business.

CHAPTER THREE

Skip the office space, for now

Let's be honest

Most of us love the idea of having an office. To many of us, having our very own offices says, " I have arrived". It is part of the whole " I am in business for real" thing. We love to say to our friends " come by the office", or " Our office is located on XYZ Street.

Hey, I am not judging, I have been there, done that. My story is one that begins with leasing I could not afford, not even a little bit, and ends with me and my team getting evicted from said offices in the most unconventional manner possible.

In this chapter, I will explain why I think that unless your industry requires it, it might not be all that important to start out by leasing expensive office spaces. At least not till you have enough customers and revenues to justify the added expense.

Unless the law says so

All major industries have some kind of regulatory framework. In some specific industries, the law clearly states that all practitioners must maintain a commercial location, whether an office space, warehouse or retail storefront. I mean, you cannot possibly operate an OBGYN out of a co-working space. My Portlandia fans know what I am talking about.

Certain industries, even by law have specifications one must adhere to when maintaining a place of business. If this is the case with you, then, by all means, go ahead and invest in a business location. If you, however, just want an office location just so folks will take you more seriously, then I would recommend changing course. Sure, having your own office makes you look legit, but at least in my experience, this does very little to grow the bottom line.

Now, I know there are various different opinions out there as it relates to this matter, and I respect all of them. I just happen to think that you can use the extra cash that you would pay in office rent towards something a little bit more consequential to your business. Like Marketing or product development.

Remote is the new normal anyway

As we all become more technologically savvy and connected, we are all starting to depend heavily on technology and other tools to communicate around the world. This seismic shift has caused many companies to start evaluating the viability and necessity of a physical office location. Many well-recognized brands across the globe now, either have a partially remote Workforce or have opted to allow 100% of your employees to work from home.

In light of this change, companies like HP and Google have been able to expand their Global Workforce to reach places like Africa, Southeast Asia, and the Middle East. Newer companies like Invision, a well-known tech company, is one of those firms that operate with an all-remote Workforce.

As a small business owner, I think you need to carefully examine whether you need a physical office location or not. The rest of the marketplace seems to be headed towards the remote option. A new study by IWG reveals that 70% of employees globally work remotely at least once a week - and 50% of employees work remotely half the week. 2/3 of Employers Report Increased Productivity for Remote Workers Compared to In-Office Workers. Remote Workers Report 82% Reduced Stress.

Is it an ego thing?

I have touched on this quite a bit in the previous

sections of this book. My personal take on human behavior goes like this; for the most part, most of us try to seem complex and sophisticated to the people around us. We try very hard to portray an image that says, "I know a lot", "I come to every decision in my life based on careful planning and critical thinking". The truth, however, in most cases is quite different. We as humans make most of our decisions, even the important ones purely based on emotions.

We Choose to watch movies that make us feel a certain type of way, we live in neighborhoods that have a certain "vibe" to them. We even choose our future partners based on our emotions. You know, how they make us feel. And although all these may seem fine, for the most part. Going with your gut can get you in trouble when it comes to business. Thinking through whether or not you need an office space is one of those things that you want to check your ego at the door when embarking on. Sure, I think once you are rolling in cash you can always come back to this issue.

You can get that nice office space that you

always dreamed of. For now, since you're probably on a tight budget anyway, I would advise that you take your emotions out of the process, and manage with what you have so you can focus on the parts of your company that really need your attention and resources.

Your story is more familiar than you think

Most folks don't realize how many of the companies we have come to love, and respect actually had very humble beginnings, along with their billionaire founders. When we think of folks like Susan Wojcicki and Walt Disney, many don't realize that they started their companies small, and with the help of others grew them to become the giant corporations we all admire today. So, let's take a look at some of the biggest companies in the world that were actually started in garages.

Companies That Were Started in A Garage

Disney

The Iconic media giant actually had very humble

beginnings. Walt Disney and his brother Roy initially worked on Alice Comedies, part of Alice's Wonderland, in their uncle's garage in Los Angeles back in 1923.

Walt Disney's first film studio I Source: Razsl

Harley Davidson

Founded by two childhood friends, William Harley, and Arthur Davidson, this iconic American brand had very humble beginnings. The two founders built their first motor-powered bicycle out of a wooden shed. The two formally launched the brand in 1903. Harley Davidson now has a market value of over $10 billion.

Mattel

The marker of the world-famous Barbie doll was initially launched as a picture-frame company in 1945. The company started operating out of a garage in

Southern California. The founders, Harold Matson and Elliot and Ruth Handler, started using their leftover materials, to creating dollhouses. They pivoted to becoming a toy manufacturer when their dolls outsold their picture frames. Mattel today is the largest toy-making company in the world and is worth $10 billion.

Ruth Handler, one of the founders of Mattel

These are just a few of very successful companies that were started out of a garage. There are many others, some you may already know. I am talking about firms like Apple, which was started out of a garage by Steve

Wozniak and Steve Jobs. the pair assembles their first computers out of Job's parent's garage in Cupertino, California.

CHAPTER FOUR

Looks like we need a plan

There is no substitute for a good plan

To some people, planning, or rather writing up a

business plan may seem like a waste of time. But I assure you, in business, in life, and everything that we do, it helps to have a solid plan. Back in the day, the general consensus was that you had to have a business plan to get anyone serious to talk to you. The bank wanted to see a business plan before they gave you a loan.

Investors wanted to know you had a plan, preferably the plan was written down somewhere. At some point, things changed. Perhaps it's because we have all become accustomed to so many stories of folks who have built great businesses without a business plan.

Sure, there are some out there who have found great success without having a solid sense of direction when they first launched their companies. I, on the other hand, happen to think that to find success, we have to know what we plan to do, and how we plan to do it.

A plan for this, a plan for that

A business plan is essentially your roadmap to

success. And I mean a detailed business plan. One that includes a plan to raise funds for your business, and a well-thought-out, robust marketing plan. Not only will you need a business plan when trying to access capital, or when looking to secure a business loan, you will need a plan to keep yourself on track and to share with your business partners and employees.

My personal feelings about planning in business is that you can never have too many plans. I go a step beyond the standard business plan. I craft plans for all aspects of my business. I create plans for sales, recruiting, and even product development. I always use my budget as the foundation of all the plans I create.

Elements of an effective business plan

Executive summary- The Executive summary is the short version of your entire business plan. It boils everything down into brief easy-to-digest points. It's a birds-eye view of everything that is included in your plan. It can serve as a sort of Elevator pitch to investors, lenders and potential partners. It is recommended that you craft your Executive summary last so as to include all the important points that are laid out in your overall plan.

Below, you'll find a sample executive summary from Coffee House Inc. Its executive summary focuses on the value proposition of the business. Here's what the company wrote in its plan:

"Market research indicates that an increasing number of consumers in our city are interested in the experience of coffee. However, there isn't a viable place for them to meet and learn locally. Instead, they only have access to fast coffee. Coffee House Inc. provides a place for people to enjoy fresh-ground beans and truly enjoy their cup.

"Coffee House Inc. provides a hub for a subculture of coffee, offering customers a place to purchase their own coffee-grinding supplies in addition to enjoying the modern atmosphere of a coffee house.

"The founders of Coffee House Inc. are coffee aficionados with experience in the coffee industry and connections to sustainable growing operations. With the experience and expertise of the Coffee House team, a missing niche in town can be fulfilled."

Company overview- As the name suggests, this part of your business plan should tell people what your company is all about. Describe your company and what it does. Here you can include the origin story of your organization-When you formed your company and the reason why you started your firm. Include your mission and vision statements as well as your values as a company. You can also attempt to answer these questions:

- What is the business model? (What are your products and revenue sources? Who are your intended customers?)
- Do you have unique business relationships that offer you an advantage?
- Where are you located?
- Who are the founders and owners?
- What is the legal structure?
- What is your projected growth?

Market analysis-Provide an overview of your entire market as a whole. Describe your competition and let folks know how you fit into your market and why customers would choose your products and services over that of your competitors. Feel free to include information about your core target market, ideal customer profiles, and any other pertinent information gleaned from your market research activities. Provide data on future opportunities and market trends in your industry.

For instance*, Coffee House Inc. recognizes that there is a* *wide trend toward "slow" food and the idea of experiencing life. On top of that, Coffee House surveyed its city and found no local coffee houses that offered fresh-ground beans or high-end accessories for do-it-yourselfers.*

Coffee House can create an ideal customer identity. The ideal customer is a millennial or younger member of Gen X. He or she is a professional and interested in experiencing life and enjoying pleasures.

The ideal customer probably isn't wealthy but is middle class and has enough disposable income to have a hobby like coffee. Coffee House appeals to professionals who work (and maybe live) in the downtown area. They meet their friends for a good cup of coffee but also want the ability to make good coffee at home.

Organization and management - This part of your business plan should be used to show folks who the members of your management team are. Most investors want to know you have an experienced, competent team to help grow your business.

Be sure to highlight the expertise and qualifications of each member of the team in your business plan. Tell the world about any special relationships or connections members of your management team have with trade groups, industry suppliers, financial institutions, etc.

Sales strategies - Your sales strategy should spell out how you plan to raise cash and drive your business towards profitability. This is where you let the world know how you plan to cover your expenses and return cash to investors, and how your pricing and sales of your product and/or services can do that.

Provide details about current sales strategies, and any marketing initiatives you look to implement in the future. Include all aspects of marketing including your digital and traditional marketing efforts.

Your sales strategy section should also include information on your web development efforts and your search engine optimization plan. Let investors, lenders, and partners know how you plan to increase revenue with your sales and marketing infrastructure on an ongoing basis.

Funding requirements - Provide details about your funding needs here. Use this section to spell out how much cash your startup needs to get to a specific point in your growth expectations as a company. For example, do you need $120,000 to develop your fist product and hire your initial sales team? or do you need $30,000 to complete your latest round of brand awareness and marketing needs? Create a detailed timeline as well, setting clear expectations for your potential investors.

For instance, it can cost between $200,000 and $500,000 to open a coffee house, and profit margins can be between 7% and 25%, depending on costs. A successful business in the coffee industry can see revenues of as much as $1 million a year by the third year, according to the Chronicle.

Some of the things Coffee House Inc. would include in its timeline are locating premises, obtaining food handlers' permits and business licenses, arranging regular product supply, and getting the right insurance. The best- and worst-case scenarios for how long this will take depends on state and local regulations.

No matter your business, you should get an idea of what steps you need to follow and how long they typically take to complete. Add it all into your timeline.

Financial projections - Finally, the last section of your business plan should include financial projections. Your forward-looking projections should be based on information about your revenue growth and market trends. You want to be able to use information about what's happening, combined with your sales strategies, to create realistic projections that let others know when they can expect to see returns.

If you're looking to accurately analyze your financial statement, income statement, loss statement, cash flow statement, and balance sheet while projecting future cash flow, you may want to consider using accounting software like Quickbooks from Intuit.

Utilizing accounting software will allow you to recognize your deficiencies, acknowledge your strengths, and craft a detailed financial plan. Doing so can increase your likelihood of securing a favorable business loan.

Build a plan with these tools

Over the years, I have tried a few of the products out there needed to build robust, dynamic business plans. Below, I share a few that I find to do the job, and at an affordable rate. These platforms, I feel all have the right mix of features to help any small business owner create stunning business plans without the need for any prior experience or expertise.

Liveplan

www.liveplan.com

Overview

From idea to business. Quickly document different business ideas in a beautiful visual format with the LivePlan One-Page Pitch. Collaborate with your team. Test the numbers. Build your plan and pitch for funding. Track your progress.

Pricing

Plans start at $11.65/mo.

Features

Step-by-Step Instructions

500+ Samples & Examples

Business Plan Template

Industry Benchmarks

Financial Forecasting

Sales Forecasting

Professional Documents

Enloop

www.enloop.com

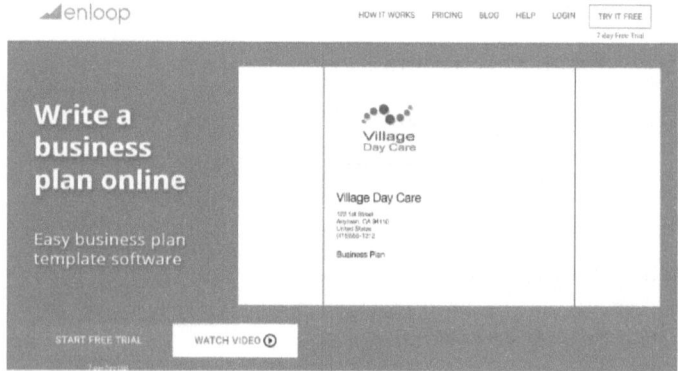

Overview

Enloop is an easy, online business plan writing software that's smart, simple and fast.

Pricing

Plans start at $39.95/mo.

Adaptive insights

www.adaptiveinsights.com

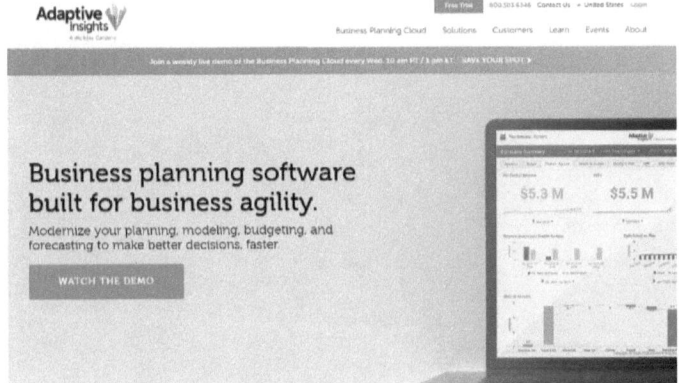

Overview

Everything you need for continuous and comprehensive financial planning, reporting, and analysis. Produce accurate budgets quickly and easily with confidence. Get more insights faster. Deliver stunning reports in minutes. Collaborate across the enterprise from anywhere—by web, mobile, and Excel.

Pricing

Free trial available

VENTURE: A SIMPLE GUIDE TO HELP YOU SURVIVE YOUR FIRST YEAR IN BUSINESS

CHAPTER FIVE

Raising capital for your startup

Be open-minded

Most investors, whether equity or debt, will require that the company, your company hit certain milestones in order to continue to receive funding. Any typical investor-to-startup arrangement will not be a lump sum funding deal. As an entrepreneur seeking funding, you must be prepared for these types of flexible propositions.

Know that if you are embarking on a series A or Angel round, you are far from getting rich. Don't get me wrong, you will be rich on paper, but any meaningful change to your actual net worth will occur after you have built a profitable business and engaged in a proper exit. One that clearly stipulates cash for you.

Startup-ing ain't what it used to be

You hear people say all the time that "The American dream is slipping away". As grim as this statement may seem to some, I actually think there is some truth to it. Let's face it, there used to be far more economic opportunities in this country. " Lifting yourself up by your bootstraps" used to be an actual thing. In the early to mid-'90s, before the dot com fiasco, raising capital for your startup was a piece of cake.

Investors, both private and institutional, were more than happy to throw piles of cash at any idea that made some kind of sense. All you needed was a plan and the passion to make it happen. Most of the tech Billionaires we know and love today, some I have already mentioned in this book, got their start during that time. With that said, the 21st century does have its advantages.

For one, we are all more connected today than we ever have been. Mobile technology and social media are two technological advancements, along with the Skypes and Slacks of the world that have made it super easy to find partners and collaborators all over the world. These are all great, but access to funds, Cold cash used to be easier.

Never too early to look for funding

When most of us think of raising capital, we think of the more institutionalized version. The more professional, meet with guys and gals in suits type of deals. We think about having to have a well-polished elevator pitch, with professionally designed slides, and the whole nine. Sure, you will probably want to get those items ready while you build your business and refine what it is that you are doing.

You will want to do this so that when the time comes to approach deep-pocketed investors, you will be ready. In the meantime, I want you to know that it is never too early to raise cash for your business. The question is: Where will the cash come from? There are many ways to think about the whole " Raising capital" thing, but before I get to that, I want you to also know that regardless of how low your startup costs are, or you think will be, you are still going to need money to grow this business.

So back to my earlier point. In the early stages of your business, you can have a dynamic view of where your funding can come from. You can approach friends and family, your own savings, etc.

Sources of Startup capital

According to business consulting firm BDC, below are a few sources of initial capital for your startup.

Personal investment - When starting a business, your first investor should be yourself—either with your own cash or with collateral on your assets. This proves to investors and bankers that you have a long-term commitment to your project and that you are ready to take risks.

Love money -This is money loaned by a spouse, parents, family or friends. Investors and bankers consider this as "patient capital", which is money that will be repaid later as your business profits increase.

When borrowing love money, you should be aware that:

Family and friends rarely have much capital
They may want to have equity in your business
A business relationship with family or friends should never be taken lightly

Business incubators - Business incubators (or "accelerators") generally focus on the high-tech sector by providing support for new businesses in various stages of development. However, there are also local economic development incubators, which are focused on areas such as job creation, revitalization and hosting and sharing services.

Commonly, incubators will invite future businesses and other fledgling companies to share their premises, as well as their administrative, logistical and technical resources. For example, an incubator might share the use of its laboratories so that a new business can develop and test its products more cheaply before beginning production.

Generally, the incubation phase can last up to two years. Once the product is ready, the business usually leaves the incubator's premises to enter its industrial production phase and is on its own.

Businesses that receive this kind of support often operate within state-of-the-art sectors such as biotechnology, information technology, multimedia, or industrial technology.

Government grants and subsidies - Government agencies provide financing such as grants and subsidies that may be available to your business. The Canada Business Network website provides a comprehensive listing of various government programs at the federal and provincial level.

Criteria

Getting grants can be tough. There may be strong

competition and the criteria for the awards are often stringent. Generally, most grants require you to match the funds you are being given and this amount varies greatly, depending on the granter. For example, a research grant may require you to fund only 40% of the total cost.

Generally, you will need to provide:

- A detailed project description
- An explanation of the benefits of your project
- A detailed work plan with full costs
- Details of relevant experience and background on key managers
- Completed application forms when appropriate

Most reviewers will assess your proposal based on the following criteria:

- Significance

- Approach
- Innovation
- Assessment of expertise
- Need for the grant

Some of the problem areas where candidates fail to get grants include:

- The research/work is not relevant
- Ineligible geographic location
- Applicants fail to communicate the relevance of their ideas
- The proposal does not provide a strong rationale
- The research plan is unfocused
- There is an unrealistic amount of work
- Funds are not matched

Angels - Angels are generally wealthy individuals or retired company executives who invest directly in small firms owned by others. They are often leaders in their own field who not only contribute their experience and network of contacts but also their technical and/or management knowledge. Angels tend to finance the early stages of the business with investments in the order of $25,000 to $100,000. Institutional venture capitalists prefer larger investments, in the order of $1,000,000.

In exchange for risking their money, they reserve the right to supervise the company's management practices. In concrete terms, this often involves a seat on the board of directors and an assurance of transparency.

Fundraising Checklist

Regardless of which avenues, and under which conditions you plan to raise money for your company. Whether you will approach friends and family, reach out to potential investors via Crowdfunding, or do some good old-fashioned walking and talking, you will need to nail down a few basic items/steps to give yourself a fighting chance.

Hire professionals

I cannot stress this point enough. Hire a lawyer at the very least, one who has ample experience in helping young companies attract investors. Hiring an accountant, again, with relevant experience can't hurt either. Get yourself a team of pros to help you prepare the necessary documents (Company financials and legal documents) to better communicate your plans for your firm. Some consultants can even introduce you to potential investors.

Pitch deck and presentation

When it comes to telling your company's story to investors, simple is always better. Keep your pitch deck between 10 to 20 slides. Here, try to communicate in the simplest terms what your vision is, what end of the market you are looking to capture, who your ideal customer is, and if you have already made some progress in any of these areas. Also, be sure to talk about your team and what each key member brings to the table, and why these are the guys and gals that you believe can make things happen.

Be prepared for skepticism, especially if you are in uncharted territory or you have a contrarian approach to an existing space. Your ego should be able to handle some tough questions. Keep in mind that investors simply want to make money and any pushback is not personal.

Note: It is easier to bring on investors if you have traction.

List of leads

A lead list in this particular instance can be whatever you want it to be. This can be a list of friends and family members you believe have the means, appetite and are suitable for this kind of investment. You can also prepare a list of high net worth folks with whom you may have had some dealings in the past and you think might be into what you are offering. Be sure to prepare a list of truly qualified potential investors to help make the process a bit easier on yourself.

VENTURE: A SIMPLE GUIDE TO HELP YOU SURVIVE YOUR FIRST YEAR IN BUSINESS

10 BUSINESS FUNDING OPTIONS

60.3% of business owners use personal savings to fund their business (Source: U.S. Census Bureau). But what options do you have when you don't have much in your pocket?

ONLINE LENDING
Online lenders offer speed: Application approval decision and the accompanying funds can be issued within days.

FACTORING/INVOICE ADVANCES
An invoice factoring provider will front you the money on invoices that have been billed out to your clients and customers.

FRIENDS AND FAMILY
Borrowing from friends and family offer advantages, including low- or no-interest payments and avoiding the hassles of bank contracts.

PRODUCT PRESALES
Sell your products before they are launched is highly-effective in raising money for financing your business.

SIDE BUSINESS
Business owners can use the revenue from an existing business to fund the launch of a new one.

HOME EQUITY LOAN
A home equity loan offers interest rates that are both flexible and lower than traditional commercial rates.

CREDIT CARDS
Business credit cards are among the most readily available ways to finance a startup and a quick way to get your business up and running.

SELLING ASSETS
Sell an existing asset (e.g. the non-cash-flow-producing asset like a car) to fund your startup

ANGEL INVESTORS
Angel investing generally occurs in a company's early stages of growth.

VENTURE CAPITALISTS
Fast-growth companies with an exit strategy already in place can take advantage of VC investments.

FUNDINGNOTE

CHAPTER SIX

Do not overlook these hidden startup costs

Expect the unexpected

According to the Kauffmann Foundation, a small business startup takes an average of $30,000 to get off the ground and running. And this is on the lower end, just enough to cover basic startup expenses. Once you throw in legal fees and other fees, the cost to start a business can be in the millions of dollars. While most entrepreneurs have some idea as to what to expect, or how much their businesses will take to get going, some costs can come out of nowhere and cause you to abandon your venture completely.

Costs do add up

For small businesses, miscalculating or underestimating essential startup costs could cause your business to fail. Costs to incorporate your new company, leasing new office space, and the purchase of computer equipment and other hard assets are but a few of the most common, relatively significant expenses associated with launching a new business. Launching a new venture, for most comes with lots of excitement, plus the hopes of building a viable business in the long term. The kind of business you may be able to pass on to your loved ones or perhaps sell for a big payday.

Money on my mind

I am embarrassed to admit this, but I spend most of my time recording expenses and sales figures for my business. I have to. I hate doing this, but I feel this is one of the most important activities one must engage in to be successful in business. Sure, it sucks, but I like to keep my mind on my money and my money on my mind. Now, I know what you are thinking: " but aren't there easier ways to track your sales and expenses?" Of course, there are. The thing is, I like to know about every little expense and sales trend at any given time.

I watch costs, sales, taxes, etc. like a hawk. I want

to be the first to know if there is an issue, or the minute an ongoing expense, no longer serves an important need, so I can make the necessary changes. Don't get me wrong, I use a Xero to automatically track and record these figures as well. I just like to keep separate records to help me make ongoing strategic decisions.

Don't let these costs creep up on you

In the midst of all the joy of starting a new firm, in the planning phase, you might overlook some areas of expenditures that when left unplanned-for can get in the way of success. Some of these often-overlooked startup expenses are as follows:

Theft or shrinkage

If your startup sells, or you plan to sell physical products, shrinkage is something you want to keep an eye on. Theft or shrinkage costs retailers an estimated $45 billion per year in the U.S. alone. There are other kinds of businesses that can fall victim to shrinkage other than retail outfits. Examples of Shrinkage include shoplifting, employee theft, paperwork errors, and vendor fraud.

Then, there is roughly 6 percent of losses that can't be accounted for under any of these categories. They're simply mysteries!

If you're aware that shrinkage is an issue, you can be proactive and prevent many of the factors that cause it. It's nearly impossible to avoid shrinkage altogether, but you should be able to mitigate it enough that it doesn't significantly impact your company's bottom line.

Payroll

Whether you plan to lease office space or work out of your home, I strongly recommend that you make plans to pay yourself on a regular basis. It is best to pay yourself a living wage, that is to say, a wage with which you can cover your personal obligations.

You will also want to work into your financial projections and/or request for outside funding, payroll for any full-time or part-time employees you plan to bring on.

Marketing / Promotion

An often-overlooked expense. I am a big believer in the whole idea of paid marketing. Perhaps it's because I suck at peer-to-peer promotion. I am still not very sure how to generate a big-enough buzz for a product or service, using just my network of family and friends. I promote every venture I am ever a part of the old-fashioned way; by paying for radio spots, Facebook Ads, Twitter Ads, etc.

I encourage any entrepreneur to make provisions for a decent marketing budget when launching a new service or product within an existing business. Give yourself a fighting chance to get the word out about your new offering as quickly and sizably as possible. I am by no means against the other free kinds of promotions. Nope! I just want you to prepare yourself to run various kinds of marketing campaigns, including paid ones.

Research & Development

Some might not feel as strongly about this point as others. I guess the degree to which you think having an R&D budget is important depends on the type of business you are in or your unique circumstances. Here, I tend to go with the "R&D is important" crowd. As you grow your business, you will want to look for areas, unrelated to your core business, where you can add value to your existing line of products or develop some peripheral sources of revenue.

For such exploratory endeavors, one can allocate a portion of their overall startup budget. You can use these funds to develop a new product line or to buy the assets of a competitor(s).

Administrative Costs

These types of costs, when left unchecked can add up very quickly.

- Utilities
- Computers
- Phones
- Printers
- Filing cabinets
- Paper clips
- Office cleaning supplies
- Software

Insurance

When you first start out, you might not need a lot of insurance. However, as time goes on, the need for various insurance policies increases. These include things like general small business insurance, liability insurance, errors and omissions insurance, workers' compensation insurance, property insurance, and cyber insurance.

How much you spend on a given policy is based on numerous factors, including the type of business, size of the business, industry, location, revenue, previous issues, present risk factors, and number of employees. You can easily spend $1,000 or more per policy per year. For a business that's already operating on a tight budget, these hidden costs can make it difficult to stay on track.

But wait, there is more

There are many other types of expenses that can become a pain if you do not plan ahead for them. It helps to make a list of all expenses to expect. Some expenses to keep in mind include taxes, accounting fees, Insurance, employee benefits, etc.

CHAPTER SEVEN

Build a Team Around You

Build a Team Around You

"The best teamwork comes from men who are working independently toward one goal in unison." James Cash Penney

If you want to create something larger than yourself, say a business, a marriage, a family it is impossible to create them by yourself. You must be able to collaborate with others working towards your goal to make it happen. Teamwork is a fundamental building block of success in business and can make all the difference between winning, losing or being stuck in limbo.

I have been involved in many different ventures, some have been successful, and some have not. What makes a team great is the ability to consistently, flawlessly execute on projects and attain goals. Teams like that are made by great leaders and likeminded people. In the same fashion, inconsistent and toxic teams are created by inexperienced, ineffective leaders. Finding success in your business requires finding people who collaborate to attain a common goal. To create this, in your business, we will run down the basic elements of how a great team culture is built and implemented.

Strength and Weaknesses

Every individual has their talents and skill sets with different personalities to match. We cannot all be good at every single business function. Typically, the best scenario is to match up with individuals who have different skills than you that will help you get to your final goal. When you start a business, while bootstrapping, you prioritize adding on team members according to the tasks needed to be accomplished and critical needs of the business. When my husband and I started our Independent life insurance business we very quickly realized that we could only do so much on our own. We wanted to create a significant business and in order to accomplish that, we would need to recruit new agents. If you are like us and are not an expert at recruiting and hiring, you could partner with someone who already has those skills and additionally, wants to build a business. By partnering with someone that has experience in this field, or any business process you don't have much experience in, their competence allows you to make fewer mistakes, as well as, get quickly up to speed.

Because of those reasons, we partnered with an experienced agency Insurance manager who wanted to increase the sales of his office. He was a great recruiter and agency manager and realized he was missing an opportunity, when he had to let go of candidates who were not a great fit for a career agent (agents employed by the insurance company) but still wanted to pursue Insurance sales Independently or part-time. We realized, we could both benefit from this situation. Our agency could work with the

Independent and part-time agents that he couldn't hire, helping us grow, and he could grow sales of his office using our agency sales. So, we benefited from his expertise and he benefited from our resources and flexibility in achieving our individual business goals.

On Positions and Responsibility...

To be successful in your business, all involved must work together utilizing their talents and experience to realize the big business objective or target. It is therefore important to create teams using leaders and team members delegated to work on different tasks, coordinating and working together to achieve the common objective.

Define roles early and clearly so that everyone knows what to expect and what is expected of them. Failure to do this step results in lackluster productivity and not utilizing the strengths of your team efficiently.

At our Insurance company for example, one of the job requirements for our agents is prospecting for new clients. By prospecting for new agents, I mean, calling complete strangers to set up appointments to help them with their insurance needs. Nick Murray in his book The Game of Numbers, says that prospecting is not natural. It does not feel natural, yet it's the nature and reality of the financial services business. For that reason, we have to prepare agents for how that feeling might affect them day to day and how to deal with it. We let the agents know early on they have to get on the phone to prospect. The phone calls aren't always pleasant but being able to help families to be more secure, and build a business is a worthwhile endeavor. So, we prepare them mentally for what is involved and what is expected of them. Because we define their roles and responsibilities, the new agents are therefore able to prospect daily in order to meet their overall sales goals and contribute to the company's bottom line.

In building a team, there is also a need for structure and hierarchy. So that everyone on the team understands their position and how the responsibilities of that position contribute to the big goal. At our agency we have agents that solicit clients and sell financial products and have sales targets to meet. We have managers that support, mentor the agents and keep them on track to meet their goals. Our Agency is an independent agency and reports sale to the regional office which supports many little agencies like ours in a geographical area for a National Insurance company. By having that structure in place, it makes it very clear how each position fits in the big production machine, which creates a sense of responsibility for everyone to do your part in order to win.

The need for good leadership is critical to your business success. Humans like having leaders and become dysfunctional with no or ineffective leaders. For your business, bad leadership literally costs money. A good leader sets a positive tone, has a target, creates a solid plan and strategy to execute, and inspires team members to work together to meet this goal. On the other hand, bad leadership causes stress on the team members, lack of motivation, low productivity and is usually unable to meet targets, which ends up costing money, eventually, a resource that is finite.

What are we working for anyway?

The goal for every business is to grow. To grow in profits, to have more customers, to serve customers better so they stay, to market to new people so that they can become customers. That is what all businesses try to achieve. The reason why all businesses do that, is what that action of growth, represents to our individual life, our sense of achievement and responsibility to those we love. A good profitable business creates security for the owners, employees and the community. A profitable business requires constant innovation in the marketplace. It is a very challenging and engaging process for all those involved and can be richly rewarding.

So, we know *why* we work in business, that's the easy part! The more challenging question is what to do and how.

Let's think about this in terms of working out, gym life. Most people work out because it's good for their body, or to reduce stress, to manage weight and a billion other reasons. There are those that work out based on a certain outcome they would like to see in their bodies for example body shaping, become stronger, become more flexible or fat loss. Based on each of those goals determines the method employed to meet those goals. Let's take body shaping, it requires weight training in isolation of body parts over time combined with a strict diet to see any change. I you want to grow stronger; you progressively increase the weight you lift and to get more flexible you try yoga, similarly for fat loss you try to incorporate more HIIT cardio.

In the same manner, as an entrepreneur/business owner you must communicate your vision to your team clearly so that they can understand what they are working for and what it takes to get there. By communicating this vision early on puts everyone on the same page, so that when you communicate your strategy to your team members, they can then go into execution mode.

I am always fascinated by athletes in group sports. Everyone just knows what to do and when to do it. A really good team is the team that executes its strategy the best. To execute strategy in the best possible manner in your business, you have to be able to articulate your vision, goals and strategy to inspire your team to buy in and work towards the goal.

Encourage your teammates by rewarding them when they hit targets so that they can stay motivated to continue the work it takes to get the job done.

Over Communicate to Sync

Your teammates will be more efficient, complete projects and meet targets when there is open communication between leadership and between coworkers. Timely information results in accurate, high quality work and lack of communication results in misunderstandings uncoordinated and unorganized work. Miscommunication and under communication results in time wasted and money lost. It is therefore critical to communicate your vision and strategy and do it frequently.

In my own life, I have noticed that people understand things at different paces and depth. Everyone is different, we don't know how long it takes for concepts to click and sync together in the brain, what we do know is, repetition increases the chances of that happening. Therefore, repeat yourself to your team members, even if it is annoying to them, repetition will work in your favor when it shows up in the quality of the work produced.

In the life Insurance/Financial services space, you learn by doing, *before* having an understanding what you are doing, and why you are doing it. You have to trust the process. It is frustrating, in the beginning, for those who like to get the general understanding first, then use the knowledge to guide their work. In this space you basically learn more and more as you progress in your career. Therefore, a good manager will go over a strategy over and over, ask the agent to do certain difficult tasks, with no immediate pay-off. The manager will over communicate why and how certain things, like make 200 calls a day for example, are done till the agent sees the results of this action, for themselves, and that's when all concepts, and actions click and sync together. If a manager does not communicate the vision and the strategy daily, the agent will get discouraged and quit when they have some bad days.

Over communication is very important to execute a strategy efficiently. My husband and I run a business together and every morning we huddle and discuss what needs to be done that day, who is responsible for what, and update each other on current projects and timelines. Whenever we assume, we each know what we are doing, something is going to slip through the cracks and make its way to the next disaster around the corner. So, in order to coordinate and use the resources available to us effectively we have to *talk*!

Positive Vibes Only

What is positivity? The official definition says it is the practice of being or the tendency to be positive or optimistic in attitude. To be positive or have a positive mindset you must practice having that mindset. Positivity is present in every human being; we have the ability to nurture it and grow it or ignore it or let it wither. When we have high levels of positivity, the benefits are enormous.

Some of the benefits associated with positivity are: It feels good to be positive, being hopeful and optimistic improves our mental outlook and also is good for physical health. Chances of recovery from a disability or an illness, improve significantly if a patient is hopeful and optimistic. Positivity also keeps the mind and emotions stable and balanced, by keeping negative emotions at bay.

Probably the most important benefit is positivity actually changes your brain and how it works, it expands the mind and helps the mind easily find solutions to problems, you are also able to maintain your focus longer. Positivity helps us to be more creative and create extraordinary outcomes from that creativity.

If you are self-employed, an entrepreneur/ starting a small business. I urge you to practice positivity because it boosts your imagination and helps you deal with complex business problems more effectively. You are also more creative in terms of creating products and services that resonate in the marketplace. Negativity unfortunately drains imagination, and just overall promotes a feeling of hopelessness and victimhood. It's far more beneficial to take control of your mental state by boosting your positivity levels to have a more content life

Similarly, your team members have to have a similar mental state. Positivity fosters a good working environment and increases productivity. A person who is quite negative, complains a lot is a mental drain on a team. Most good managers will not tolerate sustained toxic negativity because of its corrosive effects on team morale. So, when putting together a team, a positive mental attitude should be a basic requirement to create a successful collaborative team.

CHAPTER EIGHT

Improve on The Idea

"Perfection is not attainable. But if we chase perfection, we can catch excellence." Vince Lombardi.

The numbers are well known. 44% of all startups created in 2014 failed to make it to 2019. The biggest cause of business failure was that the market no longer needed the product or service offered. When running a business, if your business is not growing it's dying. Therefore, it is really important to keep improving on your original Idea. Most businesses look very different today compared to when they started. They kept working on the business, adding new iterations and overtime became the giant businesses that we know today.

The Case of Netflix

Netflix started by sending DVDs by mail. Netflix founder Reed Hastings knew there was a time that would come, where one could watch streaming video via the Internet. They had to wait for technology to catch up. In the meantime, began to add licensed movies and shows to their platform. As the technology improved, and as more people were able to access streaming video, they abandoned sending DVDs by mail and concentrated their streaming business.

Eventually, the cost to acquire third-party licensing became restrictive, eating into their profit margins. They realized it might be cheaper to produce their own shows. Netflix has come a long way from its humble beginnings. And because Netflix continued to innovate, they grew in the number of paid subscribers to the tune of 148 million in 2019.

Similarly, in the small business space, it is even more important to keep reinventing yourself and adding complementary products that will contribute to your growth in the marketplace. Growth is a natural byproduct of a business; the market will force you to adapt and grow. Improve on your original business idea to stay relevant. What process should you use to improve on your Ideas?

Method and Process

Your current customers are a great source of valuable feedback. Make feedback gathering a central activity within your customer service apparatus. Your customers will oftentimes be the inspiration for new features and products. They might even cancel your service because your service lacks a feature they need. Pay attention to the reason for cancellation and use that information to adapt if possible. In our Software as-a-service business, customer requests drive changes to our core product.

Our entrepreneurship partnership between my

husband and I began with our foray into the life Insurance business in 2012. We struggled to build the business with limited resources and experience. In the first 3 years we made some sales, but it was barely enough to pay the bills. Things started improving in terms of revenue and cash flow when we started listening to our customers, and by "listening" I mean taking and acting on customers feedback.

Every time we met with a life Insurance client, they asked if we offered health Insurance. We added health Insurance to our offering, and it provided a new source of revenue. As we added more health Insurance clients to our client list, we realized that some of the new health Insurance customers also needed life Insurance.

The decision to offer health Insurance helped increase our revenue by 52% that year which we continued to capitalize on.

Each year our team tries to find some way of creating a new stream of revenue, through a 2-step process;

1. By offering a complimentary product or service to our existing customers
2. By marketing that product or service to new customers who we then also market our existing products.

High Quality In, High quality Out

How do you come up with Ideas for new products and services? I believe the most effective way along with listening to your customers is to read, read, read. Read the news, look at what trends are in the marketplace and think about how your business could capitalize on changes in regulation, market needs, the economy, etc. In our insurance business, we added health Insurance because the customers were asking for it, but more Importantly, a major piece of legislation was passed; ***The Affordable Care Act***.

It was all over the news and everyone was talking

about it. Healthcare was, and I would argue still is a very relevant topic even today.

Your business should be nimble and be able to capitalize on gaps in the market.

When you have an original Idea, you must be willing to build on that original idea on a regular basis. Little by little, the business transforms and sometimes that looks very different from where and when it began.

For a small business owner who has to stretch their existing resources, I would recommend rolling out a new product every year and see how the market responds to it.

Keep tinkering and testing out new products and services. Try by creating solutions to problems and market those solutions at a reasonable price point.

Offer value and customers will exchange money for it.

Part of your business processes should involve exploring new ideas and offerings. I know an entrepreneur who part of his process is to go to Starbucks every morning to brainstorm and work on ideas for 30 minutes. Early mornings between 5 and 6 are great because there are not a whole lot of distractions going on yet. It's quiet and you can *think*.

If you can't think of anything, don't worry, practice it anyway, read meaningful materials and eventually you will start seeing needs and trends in the marketplace.

The brain makes connections with whatever you read, hear, or see. I would urge that you consume high quality productive information in order to produce quality ideas for products and services.

On Collaboration....

Share your Ideas with likeminded people, who will add to your ideas and not kill them in their infancy. Surround yourself with optimistic builders. I say builders because not only do these kinds of people see possibility and potential in idea, they will start working on putting the pieces together to make it a real thing that you can then offer to your customers.

As soon as you are able to, create a brainstorming team, in your business and meet weekly to discuss new Ideas for products/services or improvements on existing products/services and processes in the business.

Wisdom does not reside in one head-Ghanaian Asante Proverb. Two heads are certainly better than one, having a team gives you more Ideas, you can build on an Idea faster, you can Identify potential pitfalls faster and come up with solutions to problems quicker.

Just Start

The initial product you put out on the marketplace may not be perfect, put it out there anyway and work on improving it. I want to remind you that Amazon, the giant behemoth of a company's service sucked in the beginning. They lost packages, their packages took an insanely long time to arrive and sometimes it was not what you ordered. Their returns system was non-existent, I mean awful service.

They kept working on their business and improving it and have grown to be the largest e-commerce platform in the world. Who would have **thunk** it? Anything is possible when you keep tinkering, refining, building on it. If you are not growing, you are dying, keep innovating and building to survive and thrive.

CHAPTER NINE

Be Sure to Consult the Consultants

I am a dedicated DIY'er

I love doing things myself. Whenever I walk into a store, half the time I am thinking of ways to create the products on the shelves myself and save some money.

While in your private life, doing things DIY might be fun, it can lead you into a whole lot of trouble if you employ that attitude in your business practices.

In business, do not try to figure it out all by yourself when it comes to issues outside your expertise. Issues that when handled incorrectly can have dire ramifications. I am talking about legal issues, product development, etc.

Speak to an expert, spring a few dollars to rent a brain and some expertise. An experienced professional will save you heaps of money, by helping you set up your company correctly and avoid pitfalls later on.

Experience is Invaluable

The best consultants are people in the business you are in, or about to start. Folks who have experience in the Industry. They understand the business that you are in and what you are about to face. Before beginning my career in Insurance, I spoke to a lot of agents, agency managers, retired and current financial advisors, retired stockbrokers and they all helped paint a picture of the financial services Industry, how it worked and my role in it.

I was lucky that I did not have to pay for the advice. My consultants generously met with me and had a talk that was extremely valuable to me, over a cup of coffee. I got them to sit down with me, because I asked. Ask to sit down with professionals in your Industry. You might be surprised that they might say yes.

There are some professionals that you have to pay though. Your accountant or your lawyer or anyone who pretty much does a job for you. A lawyer will help you set up your business properly, if you decide to go into a regulated business, so you don't get in trouble with the law.

In Financial services, having a lawyer review your contracts and fee arrangements between your business and your clients is a critical step. Failure to do so can result in trouble with regulators, fees, fines and sometimes jail time.

Resist the temptation to try and save a couple

dollars to try and figure out complex legal issues yourself. Speak to an expert, they have the education and the experience to help you, use their expertise for your benefit. It is worth the money.

It is the goal of most businesses to create a world class service and products.

In the small business space, we are limited with our small budgets, we therefore have to be more creative in acquiring the knowledge needed to create the world class products and services. I like to put together a panel of experts, that I can easily call and seek their perspective. I am lucky to have friends who work for fortune 500 companies who work in various departments like management, Operations, IT, HR and Marketing. Since I have a small business, having an insight into how large, well respected companies are run, helps me institute similar procedures and policies for my business.

My assumption is that the large companies have spent lots of money to see what works and what does not, therefore, I can institute similar procedures designed for my small business to solve similar problems.

I have a family member who is building a medical clinic in a rural area. He has a friend who he runs things by, that runs a clinic in a city 2 hours away. His counsel has been invaluable and has saved my relative thousands of dollars on how to be strategic and structure his business.

He has given him tips on how to quickly get up and running once they open for business. Also, which insurance companies pay on-time and are easy to work with, and how to join an Insurance network. By getting this information, he is able to capitalize on his experience and avoid some of the pitfalls that he wouldn't have known about or seen coming had he not had that conversation.

Speaking to a consultant helps you implement the best practices in the Industry by using their theoretical and practical experience. It also helps you to be more creative and expand your thinking on how to structure your business processes.

CHAPTER TEN

Here is what you need

Tools of the trade

Every craftsman or every artist need tools. Tools make their work come alive. Without tools, even the most talented engineer or sculpture will fail to deliver their best work. Being in business is no different. You need the tools and resources to help you build your business, and sometimes even to save it from going under.

Over the last ten years or so in business for myself, I have been able to check out various resources. Resources that I use to manage my businesses. In this chapter, I will point to specific tools, resources, and software applications you can use to execute some of the ideas I have shared in this book.

Below are a few resources to assist you in managing your firm's finances, Payroll, loans, and so much more:

Accounting Software

Here are two of my favorite small business accounting software platforms.

Xero

www.xero.com

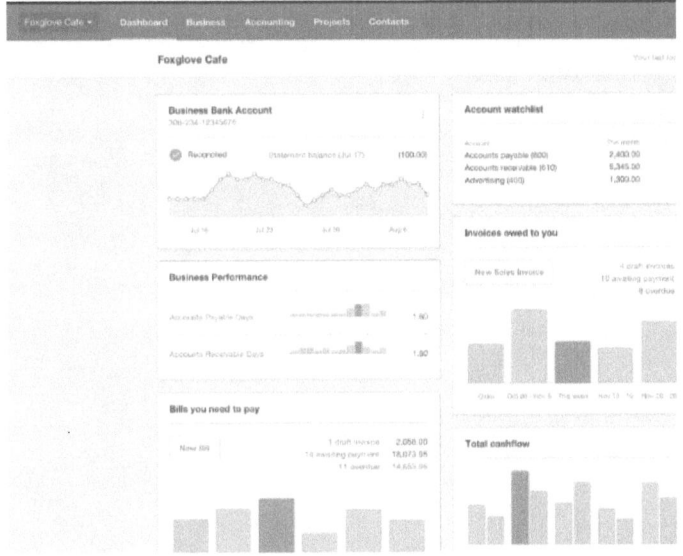

Overview

Award-winning online accounting software designed for small business owners and accountants. Available on any computer or mobile device with an internet connection. Business finances and cashflow are updated in real time. Imports transactions from bank accounts. Unlimited user logins. Integrates with over 600 3rd-party business applications. Supports multiple currencies. Data is accessible through a single ledger, allowing accountants and clients to collaborate around finances.

Bench

www.bench.co

Overview

Bench is for small business owners who don't have the time to do their own bookkeeping. Every month, Bench turns your data into tax-ready financial statements. You can monitor your business's financial health, download your financial statements, and chat with your team any time via the Bench app. And at the end of the year, Bench provides you with everything you (or your CPA) will need to file your taxes.

Small business lenders

These are financial institutions and platforms from which you can get easy access to small business loans and startup capital. I have personally used these platforms in the past, and still work with ones like Kabbage and Loanbuilder.

Most small business lenders will require that you have been in business for at least a year. These guys are no different, and some have their own revenue thresholds that a business must meet in order to qualify for a loan. My favorite is Kabbage. This is because they offer a revolving credit line instead of just a straight up loan. So, you can access more funds as long as you pay them back.

Kabbage

www.kabbage.com

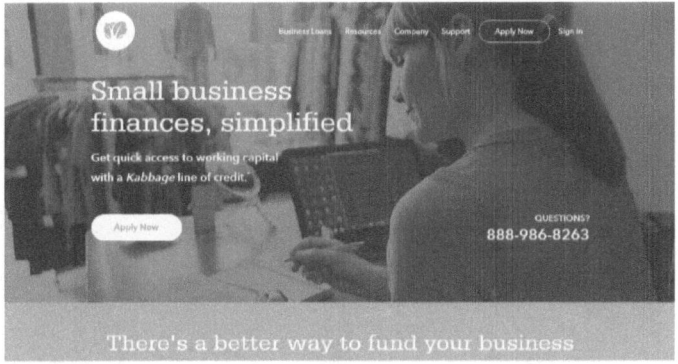

Overview

Kabbage offers up to $250,000 for a short-term line of credit that's one of very few short-term funding options that offers monthly (not daily or weekly) repayments. That said, for their 6- and 12-month lines of credit, Kabbage will frontload your interest—ranging from 1.5% to 10%—to your first 2 to 6 months of repayment, then rates will fall to 1.25% for remaining repayment months. Their 18-month line of credit will have a flat monthly fee of 1.25% to 3.25% for every month but will carry prepayment fees.

Fundbox

www.fundbox.com

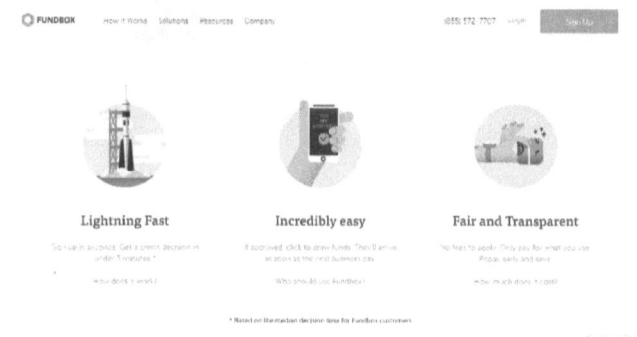

Overview

Fundbox, an online lender that offers invoice financing and lines of credit, is best suited to entrepreneurs who need to quickly fill a cash-flow gap. Fundbox may be a good option for your business if you:

Have many unpaid customer bills: With Fundbox's invoice financing, you can borrow up to $100,000 and get 100% of the value of invoices that you're waiting for customers to pay.

Loan amount:

- $1,000 to $100,000

- APR: 10.1% to 78.6% for invoice financing; 10.1% to 79.8% for line of credit

EASY TO QUALIFY

With the invoice financing option, Fundbox requires $50,000 minimum revenue with at least three months of invoicing history in online accounting or bookkeeping software that can link to Fundbox, such as QuickBooks, FreshBooks, Xero, Harvest, Clio, InvoiceASAP, Sage One, Kashoo or Jobber.

To qualify for the line of credit, borrowers need to be in business for at least three months, have a minimum annual revenue of $50,000, and have a business checking account.

PayPal Working Capital

www.paypal.com/workingcapital/

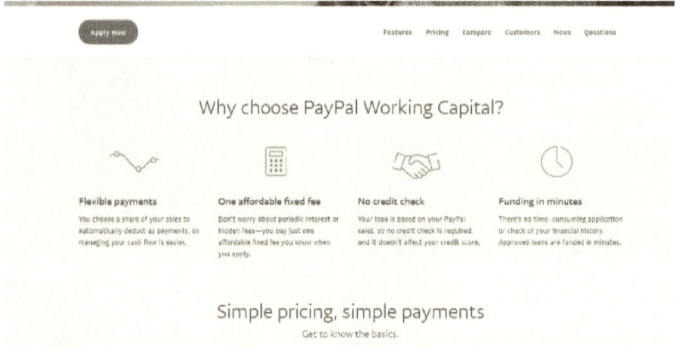

Overview

This option is available only if your business uses PayPal to process customer payments. I find this option to be the most hassle-free. You choose how much you want to pay back against your loan for each transaction and they do the rest. You will be automatically paying back the loan as you conduct business. Your loan is based on your PayPal transaction volume, so no credit check is required. Approved loans are funded instantly, no need to wait.

Pay as you grow with PayPal Working Capital

- Flexible payments
- One affordable fixed fee
- No credit check
- Funding in minutes

LoanBuilder

www.loanbuilder.com

Why a LoanBuilder Loan?
LoanBuilder simplifies and takes the mystery out of applying for a loan that's right for your business. Wouldn't you rather spend your time on growing your business?

Overview

LoanBuilder is a subsidiary of PayPal that merged with Swift Capital and a few other alternative lenders to provide business owners with a unique alternative lending experience. Business owners can prequalify and then build their loan with their own terms and rates, depending on the financial stability of the business. It provides an online-first approach to lending, although business owners can also apply for loans over the phone by talking to a LoanBuilder specialist.

Businesses can apply for loans ranging from $5,000 to $500,000 on terms ranging from 13 to 52 weeks. There are no additional fees for origination or early repayment, but there is a $20 returned item fee. The loan is structured on a fixed interest fee per payment, with payment debited weekly from business checking accounts. This means businesses can automatically pay loans back without worrying about sending payment in. These are standard term loans, as LoanBuilder doesn't provide information on varying loan types like invoice financing, equipment financing or lines of credit.

Customer management platforms

A good dependable Customer relationship management (CRM) platform is hard to find. Sure, there are hundreds on the market, but it is often hard to find one that works for your specific situation. Below are two that I have found to be affordable and versatile enough to get you started in any line of business.

Podio

www.podio.com

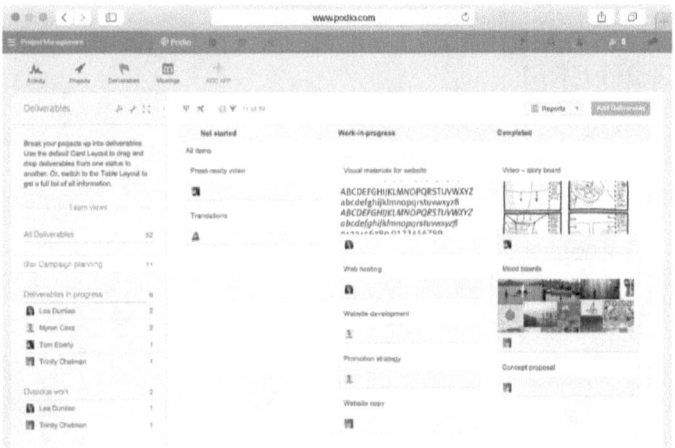

Overview

Podio is the new way to organize, communicate and get work done. More than 500,000 organizations use Podio to run projects and company departments. This includes everyone from small growing companies using Podio to run their entire businesses to innovative teams in enterprises. Podio speeds communication and provides the transparency and accountability needed for efficient teamwork, by enabling people to organize and track work in one easy-to-use place.

Zoho CRM

www.zoho.com/crm/

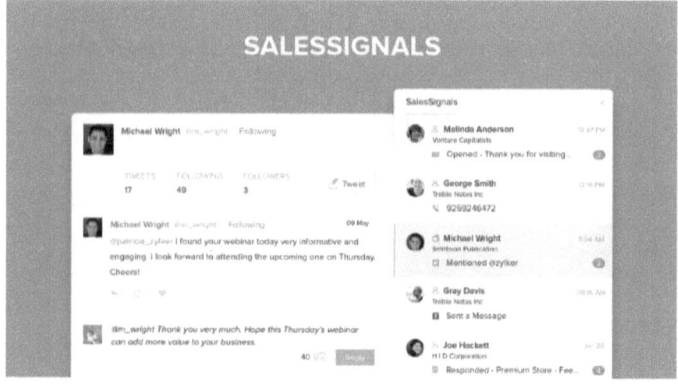

Overview

I like Zoho CRM because it is versatile and affordable. The platform empowers small to large-sized organizations with a complete customer relationship lifecycle management solution for managing organization-wide Sales, Marketing,

Customer Support & Service and Inventory Management in a single business system.

Features

- Calendar/Reminder System
- Document Storage
- Email Marketing
- Internal Chat Integration
- Lead Scoring
- Marketing Automation Integration

Starting Price $12.00/month/user

Co-working spaces

I currently do not work out of a co-working space. I have in the past though. I have tried a few companies and later decided to run my companies out of my home. That being said, here are a couple of spots that work best when you are first starting out in business.

WeWork

https://www.wework.com

Whether you're an established enterprise or a growing startup, discover spaces that inspire your people's most meaningful and impactful work. WeWork provides you with the space, community, and services you need to make a life, not just a living.

Workspace options:

Headquarters by WeWork
A standalone, private office in a location dedicated to your team (no shared spaces). Includes just the essentials with preconfigured layouts, and basic amenities.

Best for:

- Teams of 20-250+
- Primary headquarters
- Complete autonomy

Office Suites

An upgraded private office with access to premium shared spaces and amenities. Includes your own meeting rooms, lounges, and executive offices dedicated to your team.

Best for:

- Team of 25+
- Large satellite office
- Regional headquarters

Private Office

Starting at $450/month
Enclosed, lockable offices can accommodate teams of any size. Move-in ready, with desks, chairs, and filing cabinets.

Best for:

- Companies of 1-100+
- Satellite and established teams

- Autonomy within community

Shared Workspace

Starting at $200/month
Choose a flexible hot desk in an open space or a permanent dedicated desk in a shared office. You'll get access to premium amenities with a guaranteed spot to plug in and get to work.

Best for:

- Startups and small companies
- Freelancers and consultants
- Remote workers

Regus

https://www.regus.com/

Regus has the world's largest network of workspaces and co-working spaces. They provide modern, flexible workspace to customers including some of the most successful, entrepreneurs, individuals, and multi-million dollar corporations. Avoid set-up costs, capital investment and ongoing hassles: They eliminate the burden of property management. Add or reduce on flexible terms depending on your current needs and future requirements.

Workspace options:

Use as you need

- Rent a desk by the hour, by the day or by the month so that you don't pay for more than you need
- A cost-effective way to staff your business

Collaborative workspace

- Work in a sociable, shared environment
- Ideal for businesses looking to network

Perks

Technology

- Secure, high-speed internet available
- Telecom setup included

Facilities

- Kitchen area with tea and coffee making facilities
- Meeting rooms are available to rent by the hour

BONUS

Save for a rainy day

Retirement Account options for entrepreneurs

One of the hardest things to do as an entrepreneur is to save for retirement. You spend all day worrying about your business, your customers, and employees. Typically, the last thing you feel like doing is worrying about which retirement account option is best. Most self-employed folks I know never even think about this particular issue.

The idea is that they will build a business, one which they can sell later and retire and live off the proceeds of their exit. In this case, who needs a retirement account, right? Although, the thought of one day cashing out bigtime in your business is the goal for most of us, statistically, the truth is a little different.

Most business, specifically, 66% of all businesses fail within the first year. So, since there is a chance that your current venture will not work out the way you planned it, it is a good idea to start to save some tax-free cash for whatever comes next.

You really need to save for retirement

A retirement account will help you save some money while you work on building your business. Whether you run a solo operation, or you have hundreds of employees, assuming you provide your staff with retirement, health, and Life insurance benefits, you will want to look at some options for yourself as well.

Saving for retirement during your Startup years will help guarantee that should your business not survive; you will have some money to fall back on while you plan your next move.

You will also be protecting your family by saving for retirement. According to a survey conducted by CNBC, 34 % of entrepreneurs have no retirement savings plan in place. The top reason is insufficient income from their businesses. I am all about planning for stuff. I believe that with careful planning, one can accomplish anything they set their sights on. I urge you to look very closely at your firm's financial picture and make plans to save.

What are my options?

Well, there are many options out there in terms of retirement accounts, and some specifically created to fit the needs of the Self-employed folks among us. Based on an article written by the folks at the Motley Fool, here are some great retirement savings options for entrepreneurs.

Ordinary IRA contributions

If you work for yourself, your business income counts as earned income for purposes of opening an IRA. For 2018, the maximum contribution limits for IRAs are $5,500 if you're younger than 50 or $6,500 if you're 50 or older. If you choose a traditional IRA, then your contribution will typically be tax-deductible, while those going with Roth IRAs will have the opportunity to enjoy tax-free treatment not just while the money stays in the account but also upon withdrawing funds from their IRAs.

SIMPLE IRAs

Where things get interesting for self-employed people is in the business-oriented retirement plan options that they have. The SIMPLE IRA lets you save as much as $12,500 if you're younger than 50, with an extra $3,000 catch-up contribution bringing that number to $15,500 in total if you're 50 or older.

In addition to those employee-based contributions, you can also match your regular contributions dollar for dollar up to 3% of your salary as an employer contribution. Alternatively, you can choose to make a non-matching contribution of 2% of salary up to a maximum of $5,500 per year. That second option isn't very useful if you're on your own, but for small businesses that have employees and want to use a SIMPLE IRA, the provisions can be useful.

Solo 401(k)s

Finally, the solo 401(k) gives self-employed workers the chance to set up their own personal 401(k) plan account. Contribution limits of $18,500 apply if you're under 50 or $24,500 if you're 50 or older. In addition, you also get to make employer contributions that are determined in a way similar to the 20% of adjusted profit rule mentioned above under SEP IRAs.

SEP IRAs

SEP IRAs, which is short for simplified employee pension, can give high-income earners even more capacity to save. The SEP IRA has much higher contribution limits, allowing you to make contributions of one-quarter of your net compensation up to an overall maximum of $55,000 in 2018. For self-employed people, calculating net compensation is tricky because you have to account for both the SEP IRA contribution and for payments for self-employment tax. But in general, if you take your gross income, adjust lower for self-employment tax, and then take 20% of the remainder, you'll get your SEP IRA contribution limit for the year.

VENTURE: A SIMPLE GUIDE TO HELP YOU SURVIVE YOUR FIRST YEAR IN BUSINESS

AFTERWORD

Tequila is for Closers

Celebrate your successes

So, you just closed your first deal. Or perhaps you just signed your 100th customer. The great thing about starting a business, especially during the early days is the joy and pure sense of accomplishment you get when you hit your first milestones. When you finally start to see it, all come together. There is no other feeling quite like it.

When this starts to happen for you, if it hasn't already happened, I urge you to take time to enjoy it. Take the team out to properly celebrate. Come up with ways to celebrate each milestone. Create corporate traditions around your wins. For one, this will help boost the overall morale, and also keep you motivated as you work towards building your business.

This is the best part

I got to be honest with you. My favorite part of starting a business is the " starting" part. The days where you are struggling and fighting to get your first customers, your first sale, your first investor. I love the days when we are all bootstrapping trying to go from a scrappy upstart to a well-established company.

These are the days when every victory seems endlessly rewarding. The days when, as entrepreneurs, our passion for what we do comes across so clearly. When no customer is too small, no problem too out there to fix. When every single member of the team chips in to help with sales, customer support, etc. When the Human resource department is really just one person.

During these days, some entrepreneurs take the time to savor every win. Toast to every new customer. I have, however, met some entrepreneurs who dislike this phase. They typically don't enjoy being a nobody, running an unknown company. They can't wait to grow up. My philosophy, having built a couple successful companies, is, enjoy this time. These, when you look back, are going to be your favorite days. Because once you actually become a grown-up company with real employees, lawyers, accountants, and boards, things become mundane and repetitive.

Downtimes are inevitable

This is the case with every industry. Think of the Halloween store, for example. This is a business that only exists to make most of its money during one specific time of the year. Sure, they still sell costumes during the year for other purposes, but their business only pops during Halloween.

I bring this up to say that slow periods in business is a normal thing. It happens. I come across entrepreneurs who question the viability of their business models every time things are slow. I have seen some quit during this period. Sure, some folks plan or rather mismanage their finances so badly that they couldn't possibly stay afloat during a downturn. This is a shame because, in these times of slowed or stagnant growth, is when financially savvy operators get to pick up business assets at discounted rates.

This is when you can buy out some of your competitors. I say, plan for the inevitable slow periods. Use these times to improve your business processes, employee mix. This is the best times to renegotiate loan terms. This is a period to refine your business strategy and plan for what comes next.

Thanks

Thank you for taking the time to read this book. I hope I have been able to add some value to your current situation. I hope my insights, thoughts, and views will be able to help you grow your business.

Thanks.

ABOUT THE AUTHOR

Miss. Gathoni Njenga is an entrepreneur and author of several business and marketing books. She currently serves as the Co-Founder of Corvus Web Services, a software development firm. She is also the General Agent and founder of UES Benefits; a full-service insurance services company. She is also a board member and investor in several Real Estate companies in Kenya. Gathoni Njenga is currently based in the U.S.A, where she runs her businesses and loves to write in her spare time.

NOTES

https://www.walletally.com/main/top-5-reasons-startups-fail-according-to-venture-capital-research-firm-cb-insights.

We're far more afraid of failure than ghosts: Here's how to stare it down
https://www.latimes.com/health/la-he-scared-20151031-story.html.

https://www.cbinsights.com/research/startup-failure-reasons-top/.

https://investor.fb.com/corporate-governance/default.aspx

https://www.inc.com/drew-hendricks/5-successful-companies-that-didn-8217-t-make-a-dollar-for-5-years.html.

https://www.walletally.com/main/starting-a-new-business-plan-to-make-0-for-the-first-few-years-it-s-normal

https://www.bdc.ca/en/articles-tools/start-buy-business/start-business/pages/start-up-financing-sources.aspx.

https://www.walletally.com/main/raising-money-for-your-startup-is-hard-work-here-is-what-you-need-to-know

https://quickbooks.intuit.com/r/business-planning/7-elements-business-plan/

https://www.scoopwhoop.com/10-biggest-companies-in-the-world-that-started-from-a-garage/

https://www.tecla.io/blog/2019-remote-it-workers-stats-companies-should-know/

https://www.walletally.com/main/3-usually-overlooked-small-business-startup-costs.

https://www.nasdaq.com/article/8-hidden-costs-of-starting-and-running-a-business-cm860580

https://www.capterra.com/accounting-software/

https://www.fundera.com/business-loans/guides/small-business-lenders

https://www.nerdwallet.com/blog/small-business/small-business-lender-reviews/

https://www.loanbuilder.com/lb/home

https://www.charlotteagenda.com/35522/complete-list-pricing-and-map-of-charlottes-coworking-spaces/

https://www.business.com/reviews/loanbuilder/

https://www.g2.com/categories/coworking-spaces

https://www.wework.com/workspace

https://www.regus.com/coworking-space

https://www.g2.com/products/regus/reviews#survey-response-419600

https://www.investopedia.com/slide-show/top-6-reasons-new-businesses-fail/

https://www.fool.com/retirement/2018/05/24/self-employed-here-are-5-retirement-savings-option.aspx

https://www.cnbc.com/2017/07/27/survey-34-percent-of-entrepreneurs-lack-retirement-savings-plan.html

VENTURE!

A SIMPLE GUIDE TO HELP YOU SURVIVE YOUR FIRST YEAR IN BUSINESS

GATHONI NJENGA

VENTURE!

A SIMPLE GUIDE TO HELP YOU SURVIVE YOUR FIRST YEAR IN BUSINESS

GATHONI NJENGA

www.ingramcontent.com/pod-product-compliance
Lightning Source LLC
Chambersburg PA
CBHW032009170526
45157CB00002B/617